Developing a
Learning Organisation

Financial Times Management Briefings are happy to receive proposals from individuals who have expertise in the field of management education.

If you would like to discuss your ideas further, please contact Andrew Mould, Commissioning Editor.

Tel: 0171 447 2210
Fax: 0171 240 5771
e-mail: andrew.mould@pitmanpub.co.uk

Human Resources

Developing a
Learning Organisation

BARBARA ALLAN

FT
PITMAN
PUBLISHING

London · Hong Kong · Johannesburg · Melbourne · Singapore · Washington DC

PITMAN PUBLISHING
128 Long Acre, London WC2E 9AN
Tel: +44 (0)171 447 2000
Fax: +44 (0)171 240 5771

A Division of Pearson Professional Limited

First published in Great Britain 1998

ISBN 0 273 63254 X

British Library Cataloguing in Publication Data
A CIP catalogue record for this book can be obtained from the British Library.

10 9 8 7 6 5 4 3 2 1

Printed and bound in Great Britain

The Publishers' policy is to use paper manufactured from sustainable forests.

About the author

Barbara Allan is the Resources Manager in Learning Support, University of Lincolnshire and Humberside. Barbara has worked in the construction and computing industries, and she has held lecturing and management posts in adult, further and higher education. She is particularly interested in innovative approaches to individual and organisational development.

Barbara has been involved in a wide range of collaborative learning projects involving schools, colleges, universities and businesses in the Humberside Region. These projects have included introducing and developing accelerated learning approaches; using neurolinguistic programming in the workplace; team building and developing independence in learning; and developing learning organisations.

Barbara has lectured in a number of countries including Egypt, Portugal and Singapore. In her current position, her responsibilities include staff development and research to facilitate the development of an environment which inspires students' learning. Barbara is currently researching in two areas: work-based learning activities; and developing creativity.

The author can be contacted through the publisher.

CONTENTS

1

What is a
learning organisation?

INTRODUCTION

There is an ever increasing literature on the theory and practice of learning organisations and the aim of this report is to provide a practical introduction to this field.

This chapter presents a quick overview of some key theoretical ideas which have informed many practical development activities. The ideas from three main schools of thought are outlined: Pedler and his co-workers who have developed a comprehensive model based on eleven key characteristics of a learning organisation; Senge and his work on developing personal mastery; and Lewis's model which directly relates the learning organisation to models of learning.

Chapter 2 provides an outline of strategies used for developing a learning organisation. Chapter 3 provides a guide to the underlying theory and practical approaches for developing learning and learning styles. The important topic of accelerated learning is presented in this chapter. Some of the ideas in this chapter are developed further in Chapter 4, which focuses on individual learning and the development of independent learners. This concludes with a brief manager's guide for encouraging learning.

Chapter 5 focuses on developing team learning and explores two key strategies: developing positive behaviours and group learning. The ideas on developing group learning are presented under four headings: identifying learning styles; identifying group roles; developing communication skills; and developing goal setting and action planning.

Chapter 6 develops ideas presented in the previous two chapters and explores: individual, team and organisational goal setting; developing a learning environment; continuous and discontinuous development activities; followed by learning from other workers' experiences of developing learning organisations. The final chapter presents a guide to resources and includes a listing of specific tools such as questionnaires and development kits, and this is followed by a list of references.

INTRODUCTION TO LEARNING ORGANISATIONS

Organisations operating in fast changing and complex global environments are quickly appreciating the importance of their workforce and the recognition that in order to succeed and gain a leading edge they must develop their staff. A crucial success factor appears to be the ability of staff at all levels to learn and be responsive in their work. A key task for managers is developing their own ability to learn and also the learning skills of their staff. This new appreciation of the importance of the people side of organisations has been demonstrated through the development of the idea of 'a learning organisation'.

The term 'learning organisation' has become a popular phrase and may be used for describing a variety of approaches to organisational development. Useful definitions include:

A learning organisation is an organisation which facilitates the learning of all its members and continuously transforms itself. (Pedler, Boydell and Burgoyne, 1992)

A learning organisation has managers who create an environment where the behaviours and practices involved in continuous development are actively encouraged. (Honey, 1996)

An organisation in which learning is valued, and consciously managed and supported; a learning organisation develops and uses the knowledge, skills and experience of those working within it and around it, to change the way in which things are done. (Lewis, 1996a)

Although a long list of definitions could be used to demonstrate different shades of meaning of the phrase 'a learning organisation', the following terms are commonly found in descriptions of learning organisations:

- vision;

- transformation;

- change;

- participation;

- innovation;

- open;

- adapting;

- managing styles;

- systems thinking;

- learning;

- double loop learning;

- empowerment;

- reflection.

Traditionally, learning has always been considered an individual activity and it is often associated with particular places, e.g. school, university, company training rooms, and also particular phases of life. More recently, there has been a shift to viewing learning as a continuous, lifelong activity which is focused on the learner who has increasing responsibility for their own development.

In the 1990s there has been a rapid increase in learning and learner development and the idea of developing learning skills has become widespread. Many schools, colleges and universities now run programmes to develop learning skills; these are variously named 'learning to learn', 'effective learner programme' or 'accelerated learning' courses. Variations of these programmes are increasingly on offer to managers of organisations in both the public and private sectors.

The gap between the individual and the organisation has been recognised by the view that team learning is crucial to organisational learning. Team learning appears to be an important pre-requisite for organisational learning as it enables the learning from individuals to be shared and refined. By developing individual and team learning, the organisation will begin to become a learning one.

FIVE ASSUMPTIONS BEHIND LEARNING ORGANISATIONS

Peter Honey, writing in 1991, identified five assumptions which are often held by individuals working towards developing a learning organisation:

Learning is 'a good thing'. Improving the quality of learning by individuals will have a positive effect on the organisation, e.g. it will improve productivity, profitability and competitiveness.

Learning needs to be planned. While learning happens all the time in organisations, if it is planned then the quantity and quality of it will increase and staff will learn required behaviours rather than unwanted behaviours.

Learning is continuous. It is an ongoing process for everyone.

Team learning is easier to sustain. Individual learning is often difficult to sustain and people may find it easier to revert to their previous behaviours. Shared learning in teams enables individual learning to be magnified so that it is more likely to become embedded in the work of the team.

Learning needs to be on the conscious agenda of most organisations. This means that behaviours which support learning, such as reflection and feedback, must be valued by the organisation. Processes which should support learning such as appraisal systems, must be explicitly designed and described to emphasise their contribution to learning.

CHARACTERISTICS OF A LEARNING ORGANISATION

Pedler and his co-workers have developed a range of ideas about learning organisations and these are generally recognised as forming the basis for both theory and some practices in developing them. Pedler has developed a theoretical model for learning organisations from his work with managers, consultants and academics.

Their model provides a large-scale approach to developing a learning organisation and at its core are 11 characteristics of learning organisations. These are presented in Figure 1.1.

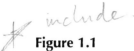

Figure 1.1
PEDLER'S CHARACTERISTICS OF LEARNING ORGANISATIONS

Strategy	**Looking in**
Learning approach to strategy	Internal exchange
Participative policy making	Reward flexibility
Informating	
Formative accounting and control	
Structures	**Looking out**
Enabling structures	Boundary workers as
	environmental scanners
	Inter-company learning
Learning opportunities	
Learning climate	
Self-development opportunities for all	

(Taken from Pedler, Burgoyne and Boydell, 1992).

These characteristics are now described in more detail.

Strategy

Learning approach to strategy – policy and strategy are developed as a learning process which involves research as well as review.

Participative policy making – this enables all organisation members and stakeholders, such as customers, suppliers, owners and neighbours, to contribute to major policy decisions.

Informating – involves the use of information technology as a tool which opens access to information and access to the organisations systems.

Formative accounting and control – enables the accounting, budgeting systems and reporting systems to meet the needs of organisational members and to assist in their learning.

Looking in

Internal exchange – involves all internal departments and units collaborating with each other by exchanging information about their expectations, needs, successes and weaknesses as well as providing clearly negotiated requests and feedback to each other.

Reward flexibility – the ability of the organisation (through the human resource department) to deliver flexible rewards (financial or in other forms) to staff in an open and public manner. This also includes the opportunity for staff to question the rewards themselves and how they are distributed.

Structures

Enabling structures – learning organisations have flatter structures with fewer layers of management. The structures are not seen as permanent but as temporary and changing in response to changes in the internal and external environments.

Looking out

Boundary workers as environmental scanners – all employees who work on the boundary of the organisation (from receptionist to research and development staff) obtain information from both formal and informal sources to feed into the organisation's knowledge base.

Inter-company learning – collaborative working and networking promotes the learning ethos and offers other sources of knowledge and learning. Initiatives may include joint training, exchanges, benchmarking.

Learning opportunities

Learning climate – involves developing a culture which encourages questioning and reflection, and also experimentation and views mistakes as learning opportunities.

Self-development opportunities for all – a range of development activities are available for staff at all levels. There is an environment which encourages all staff to become involved in development activities.

Some people consider this model too complex and too theoretical to be of much use in helping to develop a learning organisation. Critics also suggest that it offers such a large-scale approach that it may be difficult to implement in practice. However, studies of a range of different organisations which claim to be developing as learning organisations show that they have focused on at least some of these areas in their development plans. This is explored in more detail in Chapter 2.

THE FIFTH DISCIPLINE

While the model developed by Pedler and his co-workers provides a detailed blueprint of a learning organisation, the work of Peter Senge focuses on the development of personal mastery. Peter Senge (1990 and 1994) identifies five 'learning disciplines' as the basis for developing learning organisations. These are:

- **Personal mastery** – the ability to expand our personal skills and abilities so that we create the organisation we envision.

- **Mental models** – reflecting on, understanding, clarifying, and developing our internal pictures of the world. Understanding the relationships between our internal mental models and our actions and decisions.

- **Shared vision** – the ability to facilitate a group in creating a shared vision of the future and the means to get there.

- **Team learning** – developing the ability of teams to develop and learn using learning and thinking skills. The ability of the team to develop learning and knowledge generation skills greater than the sum of the individuals' talents.

- **Systems thinking** – an approach to thinking about the forces and inter-relationships that shape systems both within and beyond the organisation.

The development and practice of these disciplines is seen as a lifelong process which involves developing our knowledge and skills through reflection on our practice, whether by ourselves or with the support of our colleagues. This process of developing personal mastery by individuals and teams within an organisation will lead to the development of a learning organisation.

Like the approach of Pedler and his co-workers, Peter Senge offers another large-scale approach to developing a learning organisation. It has been criticised by some writers as being too academic and theoretical. The model discussed below offers a simpler (though not simple) approach to developing a learning organisation.

ROLE OF LEARNING

Learning is the common theme which unites all the work on learning organisations. Development activities which encourage learning at different levels within the organisation, e.g. individual, team and whole organisation, are a key factor in the development of an organisation which continually learns and moves forward.

A relatively simple model of a learning organisation has been developed by Lewis (1996) and this is closely related to the learning cycle which has been developed by Kolb and others and is described in Chapter 3. Lewis's model has four key ingredients:

• motivation;

• action;

• feedback;

• reflection.

These are outlined in Figure 1.2. This model may be applied at a number of different levels:

• individual level;

• team level;

• whole organisation.

Figure 1.2. *include :*
KEY INGREDIENTS IN A LEARNING ORGANISATION

Four ingredients of a learning organisation	
Motivation	Wanting to learn
Action	Practising, doing
Feedback	Giving and receiving and using comments on action
Reflection	Working out how the learning went and, in particular, how it could be made more effective next time

It may also be applied to a wide range of activities and processes at all levels within the organisation. For example:

- a particular meeting;

- writing a report;

- carrying out an innovative project;

- developing a new strategy;

- information handling in a particular function;

- the appraisal process.

Each of these ingredients will be explored in turn:

Motivation – this is the starting point of most learning processes. Staff who work in an interesting and exciting environment are likely to be more motivated to learn than those working in a boring and predictable situation. If staff are challenged in their work and supported in their development, then they are more likely to become involved in developmental activities. Managers with an open and questioning attitude, and a tolerance of mistakes (which they view as learning opportunities) are also more likely to motivate their staff to fully participate in work activities. Their staff will have the confidence to develop further.

Action – staff are normally involved in carrying out lots of different actions each hour. If these actions are viewed as potential learning situations, then all staff will have opportunities to examine their actions and perhaps re-evaluate them. Their findings will inform their next set of actions. Staff who are encouraged to think and take responsibilities for their actions are more likely to respond to special circumstances and vary their actions on their own initiative.

Feedback – feedback is a crucial part of learning. Without feedback there is no guarantee that people will learn from their actions. Giving and receiving feedback are learnt skills and are essential if the feedback is to be effective and lead to learning. Opportunities for feedback arise from colleagues, managers, customers and suppliers. Information technology may be used to gain access to feedback from current activities within the organisation.

Reflection – this involves thinking about what we are doing and how we are doing it and involves identifying successes and also areas which could be improved. In many organisations, the emphasis is on action and results; as one project ends, another begins. Time for reflection either during the process (which leads to improved results) or at the end of a process or activity or project (which informs and improves the next activity or project) is not always built into busy schedules. Reflection involves questioning and constructive criticism and not all organisations are open to reflection at every level of their activities.

include

✳ BENEFITS OF DEVELOPING A LEARNING ORGANISATION

Peter Honey, writing in 1996 (Honey and Mumford, 1996), considers the benefits of making learning a priority in organisations and he lists them as:

• to ensure the long-term success of the organisation;

• to make continuous improvement a reality;

• to ensure successes and best practice are transferred and emulated;

• to increase creativity, innovation and adaptability;

• to attract better people and retain your best people;

• to ensure people are able and willing to meet the current and future needs of your organisation.

The main reason for making learning a priority is because it enables the organisation to meet its goals.

A London-based finance company decided to encourage and sustain learning in all their employees. They identified eight key benefits of this strategy:

- increased competitiveness and profitability;

- increased productivity;

- unlocking potential, enhanced skills;

- increased innovation and creativity;

- greater flexibility and responsiveness to change;

- enhanced teamwork;

- increased motivation, lower staff turnover;

- improved planning processes and outcomes.

Pedler and his co-workers have described the following key benefits of developing a learning organisation:

- capability to cope with change;

- improved quality;

- higher productivity;

- attunement to customers' needs.

Examples of benefits from a range of organisations which are currently working towards becoming learning organisations include:

Government agency

- Sunrise brainstorming sessions to deal with potential problems, such as postal strike.

- Achievement of all performance management targets.

- Overcoming scepticism towards change and development for all.

Further Education college

- Awarded Investors in People.

- Doubled student numbers over five years.

- Deficit removed in one year.

- Wide participation in decision making – all staff were involved in the new mission statement.

Company operating in the public sector

- Awarded Investors in People.

- Gained new contracts worth £500,000.

- Focused staff development.

- Smaller turnover of staff.

LESS TANGIBLE BENEFITS

A range of less tangible benefits are also frequently referred to by workers developing learning organisations:

- integrated culture;

- goal congruence;

- organisational self-renewal;

- whole organisation empowerment;

- optimisation of 'core business';

- effective re-positioning in the market place.

These are described below.

Cultural

Organisations which are moving towards becoming a learning organisation develop their culture from a 'them and us' one towards becoming a 'we' culture. Traditional adversaries, e.g. managers and shop stewards, change their relationships towards each other and begin to work together as a team. There is increased ownership of the organisation, its mission and activities across the whole organisation.

> For example, a secondary school which is working towards becoming a learning organisation has moved its culture from a teaching to a learning culture. In the old culture the teachers were the experts with knowledge and skills to transmit to their pupils. In the new culture teachers, support staff, parents, pupils and governors are all learners with something to offer each other. They are all learning together.

Goal congruence

The use of participative management techniques to develop organisational goals across the whole organisation leads to the alignment of individual and organisational goals. This results in individuals being more highly motivated to achieve organisational goals, knowing that they will benefit and fulfil many of their own goals. Conversely, by working towards achieving the organisation's goals, managers are helping individuals to achieve their own goals. These two strands of activities help the individual and the organisation to achieve their goals in a mutually productive manner.

> In a university department all the staff worked through a developmental process which involved them in developing their departmental goals, their team goals and their individual goals. These were all developed and shared in the course of a series of strategic meetings which resulted in a powerful alignment of motivated individuals and teams.

Organisational self-renewal

The learning gained from the learning processes within the organisation helps to inform the next stages of the organisational cycle. The reflective stage of the cycle, in particular, is crucial to enabling the organisation to move forward in an open-minded and flexible manner. What has happened in the past informs rather than determines the outcomes of the next set of organisational activities.

> A private company in the south west of England employed a consultant to facilitate a strategic planning process which included learning from their performance over the last two years. This resulted in the chief executive and two directors identifying a lack of reflection on the reasons behind past successes and failures as a key factor which contributed to their current weak performance. As a result of this analysis, reflective time and activities were included in the next series of plans.

Whole organisation empowerment

Learning organisations empower individuals and they also empower themselves. Many learning organisations are able to move from being helpless victims of the external environment to flexible players in their chosen fields.

> For example, a small food manufacturing company moved from a declining production basis of a few conventional products to become a key international player in a specialised niche of luxury food products. This shift was the result of the renewal of the organisation by the empowerment of all the staff (through a highly focused and determined staff development programme) and a shift in focus (and rewards) based on innovative ideas and considered risk taking.

Optimisation of 'core business'

Many developing learning organisations discover that they re-determine their core business. This may become more clearly focused or the focus may shift. For example, the number of core products may be reduced. In the service industries, the products may be reviewed and reconstituted in a new and more meaningful manner.

> A small engineering company reviewed their core business and shifted their focus from a wide range of products to a small clearly defined set of specialist items. At the same time, they reviewed their approach to marketing and developed it into a more sharply focused strategy which included a wider international perspective.

Effective re-positioning in the market place

In some cases, a learning organisation may re-define its core business.

> For example, the food company described previously effectively re-positioned itself in the market by moving from a few traditional products to a range of luxury products.

2

Strategies for developing a learning organisation

INTRODUCTION

There is no simple prescription or formula for developing a learning organisation and different organisations take different strategic approaches to evolving in this direction. Some organisations which are committed to becoming learning organisations have introduced development activities in certain parts of the organisation, e.g. specialist units, management teams, while others have attempted a blanket approach.

Few organisations appear to be working to put in place all the characteristics described by Pedler in the previous chapter. However, the list of themes identified by Pedler and his colleagues (see Figure 1.1) provides a useful checklist for the many different kinds of activities which become part of their development towards becoming a learning organisation. It forms the basis of analysis for the first part of this chapter.

In organisations where there is a total commitment to becoming a learning organisation, these activities may be taking place at all levels throughout the organisation. In some organisations, there is a departmental or unit-wide commitment to developing as a 'learning organisation' and these activities may be taking place at this level. This is obviously more difficult to manage as the external environment (which now includes the rest of the organisation) is not operating from the same set of values and beliefs, and this may result in conflict and contradictions.

At the same time, there may be organisations which are involved in some of these activities yet with no conscious intention of developing as a learning organisation. For example, an organisation may be developing flatter structures and more open forms of communication but may not be concerned with developing their employees or listening to feedback.

In this chapter, the role of managers and leaders in developing a learning organisation is also explored in some detail. Finally, there is a series of case studies: a Training and Enterprise Council; a small manufacturing company; and a secondary school. The case studies show how, in real life, organisations take up some of the ideas outlined in Pedler's model and put them into practice in a manner appropriate to their own situation.

STARTING THE PROCESS

How is the process towards becoming a learning organisation initiated? There is no simple answer to this question. Organisations seem to start this development process for a variety of reasons, which are often initiated by:

- significant external change;

- new leader;

- clear champion;

- desire to become a learning organisation.

Studies in different kinds of organisation show that they often start this process as a result of a number of these factors. For example:

> An international chemical company started their development towards becoming a learning organisation as a result of significant external changes; a clear champion and a commitment that this route would enable them to become more successful.
>
> A training provider became involved as a result of significant external changes (loss of major contracts) and a desire to 'be seen' to be at the leading edge of organisational developments.
>
> A secondary school became seriously involved in developing as a 'learning school' as a result of a clear champion and also a desire to move in this direction.

In some cases they may start on this route without appreciating that they are developing towards becoming a learning organisation; they then find out that they are on a well-trodden path.

WHAT ARE THEY DOING?

Organisations which state that they are working towards becoming a learning organisation may be involved in some or all of the activities described in Pedler's model:

Strategy

Creating a vision:

- developing a simple and clear vision;

- communicating the vision throughout the organisation;

- developing the vision.

> A project team in a retail company was charged with developing a new vision for their organisation. This vision was presented to all the employees and as a result of their feedback they produced a simple vision statement 'quality products and services for everyone'. This vision was quickly communicated throughout their organisation and to their suppliers and customers by changes in stationery, posters and signs, and a change in their publicity material. All the managers and supervisors began to refer to the vision in their everyday meetings with people. Employees quickly accepted and internalised this new vision and began to apply it to themselves, i.e. they deserved quality products and services as internal customers.

Development and implementation of an action plan:

• developing a detailed action plan which is SMART (identifies specific, measurable, accepted, realistic and time bound actions);

• implementing the action plan. Actually doing it!

A school created a new vision '100% success for all'. They developed a detailed action plan as part of their formal school development plan with the aid of all the staff. This plan outlined detailed actions and timetables. Actions ranged from: improving the learning environment by re-decorating rooms X, Y and Z; developing a series of new courses for Years 7–9; to organising parent workshops. The action plans were agreed by the different teams within the school and then by the senior management team followed by the governors. This resulted in the action plan being accepted by everyone in the organisation who then committed themselves to working towards it.

Looking in

Developing enabling processes:

• developing processes which facilitate and support the vision. These may include: scenario workshops, group strategy and planning sessions.

A university decided to develop its vision for the Year 2000. It organised a series of scenario workshops which involved academic and support staff from all parts of the organisation. These enabled individuals to identify the student experience they wished to create in the Year 2000. The results of the scenario workshops fed into a major consultation process, which resulted in a new strategy with specific goals for different departments and units within the university.

Organisation information processes:

• developing communication and information processes so that they are open and inclusive;

• encouraging an open approach to information which is freely and rapidly disseminated.

A training company had a commitment to working towards becoming a learning organisation. As part of their development processes they changed their formal meeting structures and moved away from events which involved staff at a particular level, e.g. middle manager meetings, towards project or theme based meetings which were open to all staff who were involved with the particular issues under consideration. The Director's meetings were also opened up to observers from within the company.

Structures

Developing organisational structures:

• reviewing and moving towards a flatter organisational structure, removing tiers of management;

• developing a flexible structure which changes regularly to reflect organisational needs;

• developing flexible working patterns where employees may be moved from department to department depending on the needs of the organisation and the employees.

A Training and Enterprise Council changed its structure from a very hierarchical one of ten tiers to four tiers: Chief Executive, Director, Manager, Team Member. This helped to speed up communications in all directions. This was one of a series of changes which were designed to enable the organisation to move towards becoming a learning organisation.

A university learning support department formed by a merger of three existing units (libraries, IT and media resources) developed a new structure made up of four job families. Each family had two levels of staff and the whole structure was managed by a strategic management team of three staff led by a Director. One of the main thrusts of these changes was to develop a flexible structure which would respond positively to future changes within the organisation. The department was working towards becoming a learning department.

Looking out

- developing people and systems to access external information;

- developing networking and co-operative ventures.

A school which was committed to becoming a learning organisation developed new approaches to gaining information and ideas from outside. These included: subscribing to a wide range of external computer-based information services; becoming involved in local organisations such as the Education Business Partnership and Training and Enterprise Council; becoming involved in collaborative projects with other schools, further education colleges and the local university; applying for research funding from government agencies, charities and the EEC.

Learning opportunities

Organisation culture:

- developing a more people-orientated and participative culture;

- developing a culture where time is put aside for a wide range of development activities which include feedback and reflection;

- developing a culture where mistakes are accepted as part of the normal learning process and as a useful source of information.

Encouraging personal growth and development:

- developing human resource processes, e.g. staff development, progress review and appraisal systems;

- working towards Investors in People or equivalent awards.

Encouraging feedback and reflection at all levels and by all staff:

- developing formal and feedback systems and processes. Ensuring that these systems are responsive and timely;

- developing informal systems and processes to encourage feedback and reflection.

> A manufacturing company moved to a green field site and employed staff from two redundant plants. Each member of staff went on a two-week induction programme which included: an introduction to new working methods and the new culture; introduction to the design and operation of the new plant; development of learning skills; development of new behaviours. At the end of the induction process, each employee worked through a training needs assessment and from this developed a training plan. Individual supervisors were responsible for the implementation of the training plans and the human resources department took on a support and evaluative role in the process. Employees formed learning sets and became initiators in staff development activities. After six months, a survey showed that the two groups of staff had become fully integrated and were committed to their own learning and that of their colleagues.

Specific to FCF development . Possibly Chapter 3 ?

ROLE OF MANAGERS AND LEADERS

A key factor in the development of the learning organisation is the role of managers and leaders. Mayo, writing in 1994, has described the characteristics of a leader in a learning organisation as:

- visionary;

- risk-taker;

- learner;

- empowerer;

- coach;

- collaborator.

Visionary

a shared vision... provides a rudder to keep the learning processes on course when stresses develop ... . With a shared vision, we are more likely to expose our ways of thinking, give up deeply held views, and recognise personal and organisational shortcomings. (Senge, 1990)

Effective leaders are able to create a vision by using internally and externally generated information. Visions are clear statements which are focused and directed towards something or state that everyone in the organisation can aspire to and work towards. Good examples include: Fujitsu's 'Beat IBM' or Malet Lambert's '100% success for all'. They become a motivating force within the organisation which individuals will own and be committed towards.

Visions are a statement of 'strategic intent' which may then be adapted as required.

Visions are best developed in collaboration with all the staff within the organisation and they help to provide a way against which all actions can be measured.

Leaders develop and communicate a vision both inside and outside the organisation. Their personal commitment to and alignment with the vision enables it to become shared by stakeholders, staff and customers.

Risk-taker

In a learning organisation, managers need to develop their ability to take calculated risks and create environments which encourage risk-taking. This is one way in which their impact is likely to result in the organisation becoming more flexible and better able to respond appropriately in a complex and uncertain world.

Mayo describes the ways in which calculated risks may be encouraged in the workplace by:

• developing people by putting them into stretching roles;

• devolving financial authority;

• throwing away the rule books;

• investing in innovation;

• testing new marketing opportunities;

• creating alliances with competitors;

• encouraging experiments and prototypes.

Managers can encourage calculated risk-taking through the following activities:

• learning from their mistakes and sharing their learning;

• encouraging creative dialogue and the putting forward of innovative, risky ideas;

• encouraging experimentation.

Learner

Managers are learners and those who demonstrate their learning processes in their work are likely to encourage a learning culture in their teams. This means role modelling the following:

- motivation to learn;

- learning processes;

- asking for feedback from a variety of sources;

- learning from their mistakes;

- using activities as learning opportunities to aid continuous improvement;

- communicating their learning and learning processes.

Their learning processes are likely to include the following activities:

- developing a learning plan (annual, monthly, weekly, daily);

- organising learning opportunities (normal work activities, special projects, visits, courses and conferences);

- developing a wide range of contacts both inside and outside the organisation as a means of exchanging information, obtaining feedback and proposing new ideas and initiatives;

- using everyday work activities as a means of learning and continuous improvement;

- arranging and receiving feedback from a variety of people (both through formal processes such as appraisal systems and informal processes, e.g. during meetings of groups of staff or one-to-one meetings);

- sharing personal learning.

Empowerer

Empowerment involves giving individual members of staff both the power and the responsibility to manage themselves and their activities in the workplace. It involves managers delegating the task and also the authority and power which goes with it. The manager's role shifts from monitoring and controlling their staff to providing a lead and being available to offer assistance.

The key advantage of empowerment is that it enables individuals to learn more from their activities. If a task is delegated in a traditional sense, then the person may learn how to do the activity and may increase their knowledge and skills. When they are empowered to carry out a task, then they are more likely to make their own decisions and think about what is being done and the reasons behind it. This is because they fully own the experience – it is theirs 'rather than their managers'. As a result, they are more likely to reflect on and learn from the experience as it is 'their experience' rather than something which has been arranged for them by a manager.

Managers who encourage empowerment are likely to:

• set a clear direction;

• enable staff to act freely within the umbrella of their direction;

• delegate tasks as much as possible;

• encourage independence of action;

• encourage staff to make their own decisions;

• trust staff.

Coach

One approach to improving performance is through coaching, and managers are able to encourage this form of learning by:

• being coached themselves;

• offering to coach others;

• encouraging coaching activities within their team;

• encouraging coaching activities within the whole organisation.

The model of the coach offers ideas, as good coaches seek to develop independence in their learners, whatever the coaching situation, e.g. sport, the arts or the workplace. The characteristics of a successful coaching session are described by Allan *et al.* (1996) as:

- the individual chooses to be coached: they want to improve their capability and see that a coach can help them in this;

- the good coach tries to build self-esteem, successfully passing on the belief that the individual has the potential to go on improving;

- the coach gets the level of challenge just right, to suit the particular individual's level of skill;

- though the individual is stretched, there is also humour and fun;

- the relationship is often 1:1, with opportunities for easy personal exchange, potentially extending beyond the specific territory in which the coach is operating;

- the coach models the required behaviour, often by direct demonstration;

- the individual is often very active in the coaching session, for example practising strokes and repeating them, trying out a particular speech again and again, with variations suggested by the coach;

- the coach gives abundant detailed feedback on practice: information on what is working well, and what needs more attention;

- the perspective is one of continuous improvement: it is always possible to carry out the activity better. The emphasis throughout is on learning;

- the coach encourages the individual to reflect on their practice: not only on the activity itself but also on the learning methods used;

- finally (the real sign of good coaching): the coach knows when to withdraw – and let the individual go, the coaching job is done.

Collaborator

In complex working situations, both in small and large organisations, personal networks of friends and contacts are often very important in achieving success. These networks provide access to:

- external information, e.g. from customers, stakeholders, local businesses, competitors;

- internal information, e.g. about new ideas and developments, how people are responding to changes and initiatives;

- informal information, e.g. access to what people really think rather than what they may say in formal or public situations;

- new ideas, ways of thinking, developments;

- a variety of people and their personal ways of solving problems and achieving success;

- specialists;

- personal feedback and support;

- personal encouragement.

Managers who collaborate are able to use their existing networks and develop new networks or groups which enable them to:

- tackle complex problems;

- bring in areas of expertise which may be lacking;

- bring in new ideas which have been developed elsewhere;

- get involved in collaborative projects which need the involvement of a range of people and resources either from within one organisation or across organisations;

- develop 'win–win' solutions.

CASE STUDIES

The following case studies indicate how three organisations are working towards becoming a learning organisation.

CASE STUDY 1: TRAINING AND ENTERPRISE COUNCIL

This began to develop as a learning organisation as the result of the arrival of a new Chief Executive and a new Director of Personnel. Their main desire was to improve performance and they wanted to develop a flexible staff who were self-empowered. They used the following strategies:

Change to a flatter management structure

The new structure reduced the reporting line from more than ten to four tiers: Chief Executive, Director, Manager, Team Member. This helped to speed up communications in all directions and also lessened the feeling of 'them' and 'us'.

Emphasis on team working and co-operation between teams

All teams held regular (e.g. weekly or fortnightly) meetings. Directors and managers encouraged co-operation between teams.

Development of cross-team working parties

A variety of cross-organisational project teams were established to investigate and develop organisational wide issues, e.g. internal communications, and initiatives such as Investors in People and ISO 9000.

Formalised briefing procedures with feedback fed back upwards

The feedback from the fortnightly directors' meetings was formally fed into team meetings where it was discussed and the responses fed back to the directors. The internal e-mail system was used to encourage informal debates on current issues.

Commitment to attaining quality recognition, e.g. IIP and ISO 9000

The TEC committed itself to attaining quality recognitions and cross-organisational project teams were established to work towards these objectives. These teams initiated and developed the processes and they also 'carried a banner' for this work within the organisation.

Introduction of an employee development scheme

This process was being explored as a means of enhancing the personal development of employees.

Individual employee training plans and appraisal systems

The new Director of Personnel introduced individual training plans and appraisal for all staff. Each member of staff received an annual appraisal meeting which resulted in a training plan. Bi-monthly meetings between managers and their staff enabled these plans to be monitored and staff supported to achieve their outcomes.

Funding and time for staff to obtain qualifications, e.g. NVQs and MBAs

The TEC committed a large part of their own staff development budget to the attainment of qualifications. They also obtained government grants which contributed to the cost of training and development.

Improvements in communication systems

These included the use of e-mail by all staff, and the use of a range of formal and informal newsletters within the organisation.

CASE STUDY 2: SMALL MANUFACTURING COMPANY

The catalyst for change was a sharp drop of profits and the departure of key directors. New directors were committed to developing the company and making it profitable. Two of the new directors had recent experience of working in 'learning organisations' and they were keen to apply their ideas to this situation. The strategies used included:

Involvement of all staff in organisational re-structuring

This was achieved by a series of two-hour meetings at which the new management team shared their ideas and asked for ideas from *all* the staff. As a result, a consultation document was written and developed by a team representing all sections of the organisation.

Emphasis on team work and co-operation

New multi-disciplinary teams were established with clear goals and tight deadlines. This quickly facilitated new ways of working.

Involvement of all staff in a progress review and appraisal system

All staff were involved in these new processes which resulted in everyone having a clear set of goals for the next twelve months. Managers supported staff in their work towards achieving these goals. Successes were praised and first-time mistakes were seen as learning opportunities.

Involvement of the local Training and Enterprise Council in their organisational development

Staff from the local TEC visited the company and supported them in their development activities. The TEC provided access to funding for qualifications, networks such as a benchmarking club, and also information.

Introduction of NVQs

All staff within the organisation were encouraged to gain NVQs. This also resulted in the systems and processes of the organisation being scrutinised and, in some instances, improved. Staff who achieved a full award were rewarded with a plaque and also a day off work.

Development of a Parents' Club

All the staff in the organisation were parents and this lunchtime event enabled them to identify approaches to helping their children do better at school. The club enabled staff to develop their learning skills and also skills such as action planning, motivating skills and assertiveness skills. It was perceived by staff as a way in which their employers were committed to their families. Some members were staff who were reluctant to attend normal staff development events but were willing to come to this 'for their children's sake'.

Student placements from the local university

Four students from the local new university were offered three-month placements in either the office or production areas. They were introduced to all aspects of the company's work and then given specific projects. The students looked at the organisation's activities from a fresh perspective and provided a range of new ideas.

CASE STUDY 3: SECONDARY SCHOOL

The catalyst for change was the headteacher who wanted the school to achieve its vision '100% success for all'. Specific activities included:

Formation of a Learning Development Group

This involved four staff with a remit to review the teaching and learning of everyone involved with the school – parents, pupils and teachers. This group of enthusiastic staff quickly established new ways of working and introduced and tested a wide range of ideas into the school.

Development of a 'learning to learn' programme for Year 7 and 8 pupils

A change in the timetable resulted in an extra teaching session each week. This was used to introduce a new subject 'learning to learn' which was initially taught by a band of enthusiasts.

Development of 'learning to learn' workshops for parents

These termly events were established to make sure that parents were fully informed about the new learning developments within the school. An unexpected outcome from this activity was the development of a group of 20+ parent volunteers.

Staff development focus on teaching and learning

The majority of internal staff development events focused on teaching and learning. External experts were used to introduce new ideas. Many of the school's own staff led sessions as a way of sharing current good practice.

Working towards and achievement of Investors in People award

The school committed itself towards working towards and gaining the Investors in People award.

Management development programmes based on the Management Charter Initiative NVQs

A key decision was to develop the management skills of middle managers and the NVQ programme was chosen as a vehicle for achieving this goal. An additional benefit of this approach was that many of the school's systems and processes were improved as staff worked towards gaining evidence of their competence.

Networking with the local TEC, Centre for Learning, universities and other key groups

The headteacher and members of the Learning Development Group networked with individuals and groups who were concerned with developing learning and organisations. Many of these links came through the local Training and Enterprise Council.

Collaboration with other schools on TEC-funded projects

Collaborative projects were established with other secondary schools in the region and also the school's feeder primary schools. These resulted in continued sharing of good practice and the development of a range of learning materials which were then used in the school.

Involvement in TEC's benchmarking group

The headteacher joined the local TEC's benchmarking project and began investigating benchmarking activities with local companies.

3

Practical approaches to developing learning and learning styles

INTRODUCTION

This chapter focuses on practical approaches to developing learning and learning styles. It starts with a quick overview of two basic models for learning and these are linked with developing learning in an organisation. An important distinction between two levels of learning, single loop and double loop learning, is made and it is noted that the latter is required if organisations are to move forward in a substantial way.

This is followed by a detailed look at individual learning styles which leads into the section on accelerated learning. Accelerated learning is a phrase which includes a wide range of techniques and approaches to enable an individual to learn faster and with a deeper level of understanding. The final section explores neurolinguistic programming – a particular communication model that has become very popular in the 1990s. This model offers people the opportunity to develop their own thinking styles, recognise the preferred styles of others and to model excellence.

Figure 3.1
THE LEARNING CYCLE   *|| include in Chapter 2*

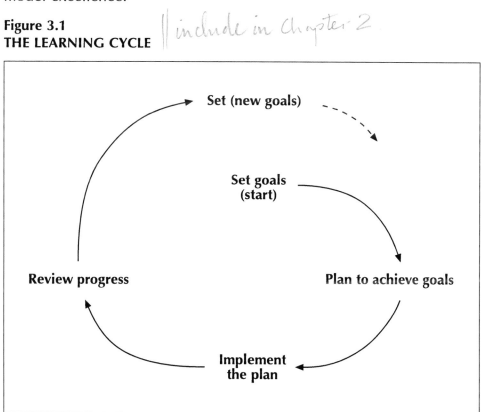

MODELS OF LEARNING

In Chinese, the concept of learning is represented by two symbols: one is for studying and the other for practising constantly. This means that you cannot say 'I've learnt that' in Chinese although you are able to say that 'I have studied and am now practising it'. This suggests that learning is an ongoing process and this is represented in the model of learning shown in Figure 3.1 which was developed from the work of Kolb.

Figure 3.2
STAGES AND ACTIVITIES IN THE LEARNING CYCLE

Stage	Examples of activities
Set goals	Identify aim. Develop specific goals. Set specific objectives.
Plan	Identify resources needed. Draw up an action plan, including timetable. Organise resources. Identify and agree performance criteria.
Implement	Find and use appropriate resources and learning methods. Take part in learning experience, e.g. visit, individual study, workshadowing, coaching, special project, short course manage time and stress. Produce outcomes, e.g. demonstrate new skills, produce a report, disseminate findings to colleagues.
Review	Reflect on the effectiveness with which goals were achieved. Identify reasons for under-achievement or non-achievement. Reflect on the learning process. Identify future actions.

Lewis and Allan (1996) have described the stages and activities in the learning cycle and this is summarised in Figure 3.2. This learning cycle may be used at all three levels within the organisation:

- individual;

- team;

- whole organisation.

This learning cycle may be applied to all organisational activities which are all seen as learning opportunities.

Individual level

- learning to use a new software package;

- chairing a meeting;

- giving difficult feedback.

Team level

- completing a project;

- achievement of monthly targets;

- development of goals for next year.

Whole organisation level

- development of three-year plan;

- analysis of sources of income for previous month;

- review of the staff development process.

In this section, the learning cycle has been presented as a simple cycle, but in reality individual learners may be working on all four phases concurrently and may be focused on different phases in different ways, e.g. a learner whose preferred learning style is reflector (*See* p.48) may be reflecting on goal setting, planning, implementing and reviewing at the same time, while an activist (*See* p.48) may be fully involved in the implementing stage and reflecting on that without having engaged in any of the other phases. Learning is sometimes a 'messy' business!

This learning cycle matches with the key ingredients of a learning organisation described in Chapter 1 as shown in Figure 3.3.

Figure 3.3
RELATIONSHIP BETWEEN LEARNING ORGANISATION AND LEARNING CYCLE

Key ingredients		Learning cycle
Motivation	*is related to*	set goals
Action	*is related to*	plan, implement
Feedback	*is related to*	review
Reflection	*is related to*	review

brief definition chapter 2.

SINGLE AND DOUBLE LOOP LEARNING

An important ingredient for the development of learning organisations is the ability to develop from single loop to double loop learning. Single loop learning takes place when the above learning cycles are used as a means of improving current activities. For example, it may result in the identification of errors which are then corrected the next time around or the identification of possible improvements in organisational procedures which are then introduced as a means of improving performance.

This contrasts with double loop learning which includes the questioning of the organisation's underlying beliefs, values and norms. This may result in different procedures or activities being introduced into the organisation as a result of feedback and reflection from the learning process. Double loop learning is much harder to achieve as it involves thinking about and perhaps challenging accepted orthodoxies and strategies.

> For example, a manufacturer of paper products reviewed its training programme and identified a number of ways of improving their efficiency, e.g. by the retiming of certain short courses and the development of a range of new courses. This is an example of single loop learning. For this company to move into double loop learning, they would need to identify and analyse the underlying values and beliefs which were built into the training programme. When this happened they identified that they were operating within a very narrow set of beliefs about what constitutes an excellent training programme and that these were 'excellent programmes involving short courses which were hard hitting and involved minimum time away from the production line'. The result of this finding and an investigation into training activities in companies in similar situations resulted in them moving away from short courses towards individualised work-based training activities and commercial open learning programmes.

briefly) include Handey et al. —

LEARNING ABOUT LEARNING

Honey and Mumford learning styles

An important concept in learning is the way in which we prefer to learn. Different people have different ways of getting involved and engaged in learning activities. Honey and Mumford have carried out research in a large number of organisations on how people prefer to learn. Their findings suggest that there are four preferred learning styles:

- activist;

- theorist;

- reflector;

- pragmatist.

These are described in some detail in Figure 3.4. Honey and Mumford suggest that we all have a different preferred mix of these learning styles.

Figure 3.4
HONEY AND MUMFORD LEARNING STYLES

This is a summary of this approach to learning styles. These are generalised descriptions and it is important not to use them to label or pigeon hole people. While everyone has a preferred learning style, this changes over time and in response to new working situations.

Activists
They become fully involved in new experiences, living for the here and now, and trying anything once. They like to learn by doing things, e.g. exercises or activities.

Reflectors
They prefer to stand back from the action and observe from a variety of angles before coming to any conclusions. They like to learn by bringing together lots of ideas and theories and weighing up the best approach. They enjoy sitting and listening to ideas and theories.

Theorists
Theorists are logical, developing sound and complex theories from their observations. They prefer objective to subjective judgements. They like to collect information to inform their theorising and may be unhappy about acting without what they perceive as sufficient information.

Pragmatists
Pragmatists like to try out things to see if they work in practice: they want to put new ideas into immediate practice and they often use the principle that if something works it must be good.

(Adapted from Honey, 1982).

A manager in a chemical company rates highly as being an activist and pragmatist but is a less well-developed theorist and reflector, and she prefers to learn by getting involved in activities and thinking things through as she goes along. One of her colleagues rates very highly on the reflector and theorist but virtually nothing on the activist and pragmatist scales, he prefers to learn by working through the theory and writing detailed notes and plans before he gets involved in any activity.

Different profiles of learning styles result in different approaches to tackling tasks and preferred ways of taking in and understanding new ideas. There is no 'best' approach and each approach has its own particular mix of strengths and weaknesses. An understanding of our own learning styles is useful as it enables us to develop our weakest styles and 'play to' our strengths.

In learning situations it can be useful to identify an individual's preferred learning style. This information may then be used by the individual member of staff, their colleagues, team leader, manager or trainer to inform the learning situation. For example, in a project an activist may be reminded of the need to thoroughly plan their actions and to do sufficient background research. Similarly, an activist/pragmatist may be paired with a reflector/theorist so that they build on their different strengths and balance out their individual weaknesses. Trainers and managers may use this information when they are planning training sessions or work-based activities to enable them to match the learning styles of their staff and also to develop their less-developed learning styles.

A range of tools is available to help learners identify their preferred learning style (*See* Figure 3.4).

mention briefly ?

ACCELERATED LEARNING

The concept of accelerated learning, which means increasing both the speed of learning and also the quality of learning, has become very popular in the 1990s. Ideas and techniques which accelerate learning and improve performance include:

- getting into a state of relaxed alertness;

- absorbing information in a paced, rhythmic way;

- using music to expand memory, energise the mind, and link to the subconscious;

- engaging the whole brain: using all our intelligences;

- playing to our preferred learning styles and developing the others;

- consciously reflecting on and learning from our current learning processes so that next time we learn more efficiently.

A core idea in many accelerated learning approaches comes from Howard Gardner, a psychologist based at Harvard University, who suggests that the traditional concept of intelligence is too narrow since it does not take into account the wider range of preferred information processing styles which are demonstrated by different people. He suggests that the following styles represent the ways in which learners prefer to take in and process (i.e. learn) new ideas.

- linguistic – involves use of words and language, enjoyment of books, dialogue and jokes;

- mathematical/logical – involves step-by-step processes, looking for patterns, rational and well-ordered;

- musical – involves music, rhythm, pitch, tone and pattern;

- visual/spatial – involves looking at things and seeing the whole picture as well as the details, able to read maps, diagrams and charts, able to understand where things are in relationship to each other;

- inter-personal – involves working with others, understanding other people's emotions and motivations;

- intra-personal – involves going into yourself and perhaps daydreaming, thinking things through in your head;

- emotional – involves understanding ourselves and our emotions;

- bodily/physical – involves physical activities and all other kinds of activities.

Howard Gardner suggests that traditional forms of learning and education are chiefly based on using linguistic and mathematical/logical thinking styles. Apparently, only 15% of the population have this profile, which suggests that for the remaining 85% a different approach to learning is required if they are to achieve their potential. He suggests that a trainer or tutor needs to take into account this wide range of approaches to meet everyone's learning needs and to help learners achieve their potential.

NEUROLINGUISTIC PROGRAMMING

The identification and development of individual thinking styles is a key feature of some programmes on developing organisational learning. One approach which is increasingly used in a number of organisations is based on the neurolinguistic programming model of information processing developed by Bandler and Grinder. This model focuses on three of Howard Gardner's thinking styles and develops them in some depth.

Bandler and Grinder developed a model of communication (which is clearly summarised by O'Connor and McDermott in 1996) based on very detailed observation of expert communicators and their model is known as neurolinguistic programming (NLP). NLP looks at how people prefer to take in, organise and access information in their mind. They have found that individuals tend to prefer one of three main methods, or sensory modes, of taking in and processing information.

The main styles are:

- visual;

- auditory;

- kinaesthetic.

This links directly with Gardner's visual/spatial, musical, and bodily/physical information processing styles which are described in the previous section.

Visual people prefer to take in new information in a visual form, e.g. pictures, charts, reading or diagrams, and like to visualise information. Auditory people may prefer to listen and talk through new ideas. They frequently remember the tone and exact content of different conversations. In contrast, kinaesthetic learners like to be actively involved in doing things and like to touch and handle things.

It is relatively simple to identify the preferred NLP learning style of an individual learner. The simplest approach is to listen to someone's language patterns and these are described in more detail in Figure 3.5. The careful observation of body language and details such as direction of eye movements and breathing patterns may also be used to identify individual preferences. These are beyond the scope of this report and are succinctly summarised by O'Connor.

By matching a learner's preferred style, e.g. through the teaching and training methods we use, and also by the language we use, they are more likely to understand and remember the new ideas. The most effective trainers are those who express ideas in different ways to cover all three preferences, so that all the learners will have access to the ideas in their preferred style.

Figure 3.5
NLP AND LEARNING STYLES

Visual learners will use and respond to phrases like:

I see that now	That looks right
Let's get this into perspective	I'm in the dark on this one
I get the picture	I can't see where we are going
It appears to me	What's your view?

and they will use terms such as:

picture, focus, image, clear, reflect, clarify, visualise, see, notice, illustrate, show, perspective, view, vision.

Auditory learners will use and respond to phrases such as:

That rings a bell	I don't like the sound of that
I get the message loud and clear	That strikes a chord
I can't hear what I'm thinking	That's music to my ears

and they will use terms such as:

audible, remark, sound, harmonious, accent, rhythm, discuss, listen, tone, ask, hear, speechless, quiet, shout.

Kinaesthetic learners frequently use phrases such as:

How does that grab you?	It doesn't feel right to me
Give me a concrete example	He is a slippery customer
She has a firm grasp of the subject	Let's work through it

and they will use terms such as:

touch, feel, push, handle, move, fix, mend, stress, sensitive, tension, grasp, hold, warm, cold, rough, smooth, touchy, pushover, contact, sort out.

(Adapted from O'Connor and Seymour, 1993).

4

Developing
individual learning

INTRODUCTION

This chapter is concerned with developing staff so that they become independent learners. Independent learners are characterised by their motivation to learn, their ability to manage their own learning process and their ability to reflect on and learn from their activities.

One of the myths about independent learners is that they 'do it by themselves'; this is not the case as these people are likely to learn in association with others and ask for feedback and help from their colleagues and others. A detailed definition of an independent learner is presented in Figure 4.1. The development of independent learners in the workplace is a core strategy for developing a learning organisation.

Figure 4.1
DEFINITION OF AN INDEPENDENT LEARNER

(handwritten margin note: Conclusion need ALL managers to be independent learners)

Motivation

Independent learners are motivated to learn. They accept responsibility for their own learning and have the confidence to approach others for help if they need it.

Management of the learning process

Independent learners are capable of managing their learning processes effectively. This includes:

- identifying learning objectives;
- selecting and using appropriate methods and techniques;
- managing time, stress, other commitments and the process of change;
- using a wide range of learning opportunities and resources;
- adapting the learning process to make use of new opportunities.

Reflection

Independent learners are able to monitor and reflect critically on how and what they learn. Through this they develop an awareness that helps them to learn with increasing effectiveness. They also demonstrate a more questioning attitude to what they learn.

(Taken from Allan, Cook and Lewis, 1996).

Staff who are independent learners are likely to find that they achieve the following benefits from their independence in learning:

- successful completion of activities and projects;

- very good time management;

- ability to cope when the going gets tough;

- find learning enjoyable;

- learn what they need in less time;

- know where to find help when they need it (and feel okay about asking for help);

- learn on their own;

- gain a better understanding of their topic;

- are more aware of 'gaps' in their knowledge;

- always be improving their ability to learn;

- are more original and creative in their thinking;

- become a more effective lifelong learner;

- recognise their own achievements;

- value themselves as an independent learner.

(Adapted from Allan *et al.*, 1996).

DEVELOPING INDEPENDENT LEARNERS

An organisation which encourages its staff to develop their learning skills and to become independent learners will be moving towards becoming a learning organisation. Independence in learning may be developed through a range of activities and processes which help staff to develop their motivation, their ability to manage their learning, or their skills in reflection.

A useful starting point is the *Independence in Learning at Work* inventory which is presented later in this chapter. This inventory is a tool which will enable staff to develop their awareness of their approach to learning.

The inventory actually measures what learners say they do and/or what learners think they do. It doesn't necessarily measure what learners actually do. Staff are asked to answer questions and for many of the questions tick one of four answer boxes. The inventory is a process tool which provides a basis for thinking, questioning and reflection. Used in conjunction with colleague and manager/trainer assessment, mismatches in perception may be identified and used as a basis for discussion and development activities. The results from the inventory may be used as a starting point to develop an individual action plan. An example action plan format is presented in Figure 4.2.

The development of independence in learning is likely to be started off by individual managers or the human resource department and to be taken up and owned by individual employees as they become increasingly responsible for their own learning.

Motivation

While some staff may be highly motivated to develop their ability to learn, others may need to go through a development process. This may be a short- or long-term process depending on the starting point of the member of staff. Motivation may be developed by organising particular events or activities, and by encouraging and role modelling the following skills:

- ability to set learning goals;

- ability to ask for assistance;

- self-confidence;

- assertiveness skills;

- ability to work with colleagues, mentors, managers and trainers in a positive manner.

Figure 4.2
EXAMPLE ACTION PLAN

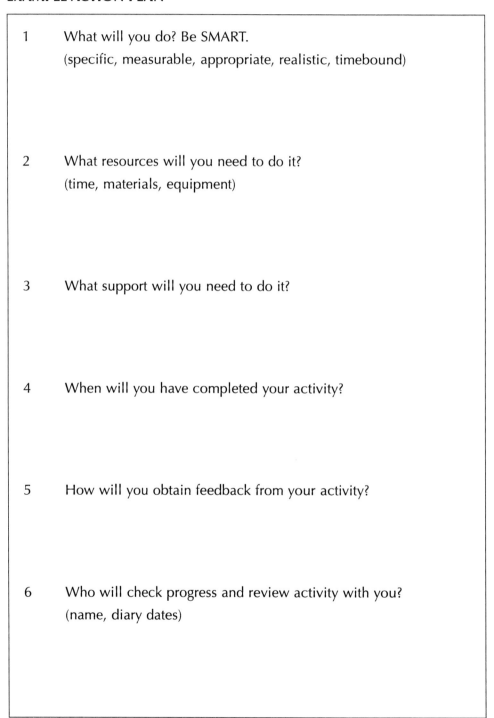

1	What will you do? Be SMART.
	(specific, measurable, appropriate, realistic, timebound)
2	What resources will you need to do it?
	(time, materials, equipment)
3	What support will you need to do it?
4	When will you have completed your activity?
5	How will you obtain feedback from your activity?
6	Who will check progress and review activity with you?
	(name, diary dates)

A key factor when developing staff motivation to learn is that they must be able to see that learning is valued in the workplace. This may take place through positive feedback, linking achievement (such as higher production figures) with learning or pointing out the successes which have resulted from staff learning. In some organisations learning may be rewarded through promotion or the achievement of bonuses.

> For example, one university department rewards their support staff by annual increments if they are able to demonstrate the development of their knowledge, skill or behavioural competencies. A large horticultural company rewards their staff with a financial bonus for the achievement of NVQs.

In many organisations, the rewards are unlikely to be financial and staff must be able to see the benefits (to themselves, their teams and the organisation) if they are to be motivated. Motivation isn't something which can be delivered through a one-off training course and it needs to be valued and developed as part of an ongoing process.

The concept of self-esteem, that is valuing the self, appears to be a key to developing effective learning skills. People with high self-esteem are more likely to:

- embark on learning activities;

- ask for help;

- cope with uncertainty.

Managing the learning process

Managing the learning process involves the following kinds of skills and processes:

- identifying learning objectives or goals;

- selecting and using appropriate learning methods and techniques;

- understanding their own learning style;

- managing time, stress, other commitments and the process of change;

- using a wide range of learning opportunities, e.g. normal work-based activities, courses, special projects;

- using a wide range of resources, e.g. colleagues, team leaders, managers, trainers, books and magazines, Internet, CD-ROMs, libraries;

- adapting the learning process to make use of new opportunities.

The types of activities which individual learners may become involved in include:

- action planning and goal setting as part of normal work activities, e.g. during meetings;

- involvement in a wide range of learning activities, e.g. short courses, projects, quality circles, mentoring, open or distance learning;

- learning about accelerated learning techniques;

- learning about own learning styles;

- workshops on time and stress management;

- workshops on life planning;

- specialist seminars or conferences;

- using formal and informal networks to facilitate learning;

- using internal information sources, e.g. library, organisation documents, other staff;

- using external information sources, e.g. library, Internet, specialists.

Reflection

The concept of reflection has become increasingly important in recent years and it is associated with initiatives to improve the quality of learning and the ability of people to perform in the workplace. The main purpose behind reflection is to improve the quality of information about a particular activity or event and someone's current or future performance. The reflective process enables a particular experience to be understood at a deeper level and this then informs future actions.

Reflection involves questioning, criticism, analysis and evaluation – either during an activity and/or at the end of an activity. It is something which most people carry out in an informal way, e.g. thinking about what went well or could have been improved in a particular activity, process or event. Reflection which is linked to the production of an action plan is usually more productive than that which doesn't result in anything tangible.

The ability to reflect and the need to develop a reflective practice are not new concepts. They are well established in initial professional training and continuing professional development practices in many professions, e.g. medicine, music, art and design and teaching. There they are seen as important in enabling professionals to develop a process which enhances their ability to learn from everyday professional activities.

Practical approaches to developing skills of reflection

The following activities encourage reflection:

- allocating time to reflect;

- creating an appropriate environment (both physical and psychological);

- capturing ideas, e.g. through the use of learning logs and diaries;

- modelling reflective behaviour, e.g. by team leaders, managers and trainers;

- using pre-prepared sets of questions to prompt reflection;

- using questions to encourage a change of focus, e.g. from a very detailed analysis to a broad picture, or by switching the focus from the task to the people involved in the task;

- using learning style models to understand and enhance reflective practice;

- practising reflection on everyday activities, e.g. at the end or during the middle of meetings, at certain times of the day.

WORKING WITH INDEPENDENT LEARNERS

As staff develop their learning skills and become more sophisticated learners, then they operate in a more independent manner. They are self-motivated, self-managing and reflective in their work. They frequently ask for and receive feedback from their colleagues, managers and others. They are good at asking questions about

- what is done;

- how it is done;

- when it is done;

- why it is done.

and they handle the answers in an appropriate manner.

As this process continues, staff are learning how to be flexible and responsive to internal and external influences. They are likely to be conscious of their values and beliefs and may be choosing to change them. They value time for reflection and thinking. The split between professional and private life may become less distinct.

Staff continue to develop their learning skills, moving to higher levels of sophistication of action and reflection. This may be facilitated through workshops and seminars. The split between trainer/trainee or facilitator/participant is blurred as all staff are seen to have important contributions to make to processes and activities. The divisions between work/learning become fuzzy and indistinguishable as every activity and event is seen as a potential learning situation.

Chapter 3 & Conclusion

MANAGEMENT STRATEGIES FOR ENCOURAGING LEARNING

Managers and team leaders who encourage learning are likely to be seen to:

- value learning;

- enable staff to plan their learning through the use of written learning plans (annual, six-monthly, monthly and weekly);

- support and follow up learning plans;

- provide staff with time, resources and support to attend development events;

- provide staff with time and an appropriate environment (including psychological space) for them to learn in the workplace on structured activities, e.g. coaching, independent study, computer-based training;

- encourage innovative events, e.g. workshops on accelerated learning, 'away days' working in unusual environments;

- encourage exchange of ideas and feedback though work shadowing, job rotation, work placements, e.g. in similar and different organisations, student placements in your workplace, networking;

- manage all work activities as learning opportunities and use the learning cycle to guide this process;

- encourage individuals and teams to identify their own thinking and learning processes and refer to these during everyday activities;

- use mistakes as learning opportunities;

- give and encourage constructive feedback;

- set aside time and psychological space for reflection;

- role model learning processes and 'think aloud' your own learning processes;

- reward learning.

Peter Honey has described 101 ways to develop people through work-based learning (*See* Figure 4.3).

Appendix

Figure 4.3
101 WAYS TO DEVELOP STAFF

acting as a sounding board	job descriptions
advertising lessons learned	keeping activity/time logs
aiming high	keeping learning logs
analysing mistakes	learning contracts
answering questions	learning from in-trays
anticipating consequences	listening
appraising	market testing
asking for advice	marketing
asking questions	meetings
audio tapes	mentoring
being curious	mission statements
benchmarking	modifying behaviour
brainstorming	negotiating
briefing	networking
budgeting	offering encouragement
building learning into the system	organising an event
celebrating success	persuading and influencing
challenging	planning
championing change	praising
clarifying values	presenting
coaching	process re-engineering
collaborating in decisions	producing one-pagers
compiling scrapbooks	project work
conducting surveys	reading
confessing	rehearsing
consulting	resolving conflicts
covering for holidays	reviewing learning
creating your own workshop	rewarding the 'right' behaviours
creativity	rotating jobs
criticising	sayings and mottos
customer focus groups	searching for opportunities
cutting costs	secondments
debating	self-assessment questionnaires
debriefing	self development
delegating	setting deadlines
empowering	shadowing
enriching jobs	skipping levels
experimenting	spotting trends
external consultants	stress management
flipcharts	surfacing expectations
forecasting	teamwork
funding development	testing understanding
giving feedback	training videos
giving itemised responses	upward appraisal/feedback
giving outside talks	using competencies
giving responsibility for quality	using SWOT
griping sessions	using training programmes
holding a promises auction or swop shop	visioning
identifying 'stoppers' and blockages	weighing up pros and cons
inducting new-starters	writing
interviewing	

(Taken from Honey, 1994).

chap Appendix include in Chapter 3.

Developing yourself as a learner

The aim of these questions is to help you to think about your approach to learning in a work context. When answering these questions, you might like to think about a particular situation at work where you needed to learn something new or you might answer them in relation to how you generally approach learning at work.

Everyone is unique and there is no 'right' approach to learning. By learning how we learn and by exploring new and different approaches to learning, it is possible to become even more effective learners.

In some of these questions you are asked to score yourself out of 10 (0 low, 10 high)

Motivation

1	How interested are you in learning more about your work?	/10
2	How interested are you in how you learn?	/10
3	How keen are you to become a better learner?	/10

Managing your learning

		never	rarely	sometimes	always
4	Do you identify when you need to learn something at work?	❏	❏	❏	❏
5	Do you plan how and when you are going to learn something?	❏	❏	❏	❏
6	If you were having difficulties learning something, do you consider a variety of sources of help, for example colleagues, specialists, books?	❏	❏	❏	❏
7	If you come across new approaches, would you incorporate them into your learning processes?	❏	❏	❏	❏

Reflection

		never	rarely	sometimes	always
8	To what extent do you question what you are told, for example by managers, specialists, books, reports?	❏	❏	❏	❏
9	When you have finished learning about something, do you think back about how effective your learning process was?	❏	❏	❏	❏
10	Do you change the way you go about learning new things as a result of thinking about past learning situations?	❏	❏	❏	❏

Interpreting the results

The main aim of this questionnaire is to encourage you to reflect on how you learn at work. You may find it helpful to work out your score and assess your overall independence in learning.

Motivation

Add up your three scores.   Total score   _____

0–10 = low independence, 11–20 = moderate independence, 21–30 = high independence

Managing your learning

Score 1 = never, 2 = rarely, 3 = sometimes, 4 = always

Add up your four scores.   Total score   _____

4–7 = low independence, 8–12 = moderate independence, 13–16 = high independence

Reflection

Score 1=never, 2=rarely, 3=sometimes, 4=always

Add up your three scores.   Total score   _____

3–5 = low independence, 6–9 = moderate independence, 10–12 = high independence

Grand total

                                   Grand total   _____
                    Overall independence level   _____

7–19 = low independence, 20–39 = moderate independence, 40–58 = high independence

This questionnaire gives an indication of how independent you are as a learner. If you rate yourself as having low or moderate independence, you could probably benefit from working at increasing your level of 'learner independence'. You may like to discuss this with your trainer, employees development officer or manager.

(Adapted from Allan *et al.*, 1996).

5

Developing team learning

INTRODUCTION

Team learning is essential to organisational learning and success, as it focuses and builds upon individual learning. Individual learning does not necessarily lead to organisational learning but team learning becomes a microcosm for learning throughout the whole organisation. Individual insights are shared and may be put into action. Skills are developed, refined and shared within the team.

Teams are able to take an individual's learning and magnify and adapt it so that it becomes greater than the parts. Team learning involves the alignment and development of the team so that it creates the results the members really want, i.e. the team goals and the individual's goals become the same.

Most of us are able to think back to a time when we were a member of a 'great team' perhaps as a result of our involvement in a sporting activity, the performing arts, or a work-based project. We are able to identify the characteristics of these teams:

• honesty and trust;

• constructive relationships;

• ability to reflect and learn from previous actions;

• acceptance of each other's strengths and weaknesses;

• synergy and an alignment of goals;

• humour;

• superb results.

Often we hope to reproduce them in our current working life and are constantly frustrated by not being able to achieve their level of energy and success. Great teams start off as groups of individuals and develop as the team grows and develops and individuals begin to learn from each other. During these processes team members undergo deep learning processes which may involve learning new skills and behaviours, and as a result develop new beliefs and assumptions. They move into a 'virtuous circle' and the learning constantly reinforces itself and moves on to new levels of learning.

Team learning may be developed through the following strategies:

• developing positive behaviours;

• developing group learning.

DEVELOPING POSITIVE BEHAVIOURS

There are a range of behaviours which support team learning. These are identified in Figure 5.1.

Figure 5.1.
DEVELOPING POSITIVE BEHAVIOURS

Wanted behaviour	Unwanted behaviour
Asking questions	Acquiescing
Suggesting ideas	Rubbishing ideas
Exploring alternatives	Going for expedient, quick fixes
Taking risks/experimenting	Being cautious
Being open about the way it is	Telling people what they want to hear/filtering bad news
Converting mistakes into learning	Repeating the same mistakes
Reflecting and reviewing	Rushing around keeping active
Talking about learning	Talking anecdotes (i.e. what happened not what was learnt)
Taking responsibility for own learning and development	Waiting for other people to do it
Admitting inadequacies and mistakes	Justifying actions/blaming other people or events

(Developed by Honey, 1991).

Strategies for developing these behaviours in team members include:

- specific skills training;

- team development workshops;

- team appraisal processes;

- individual appraisal processes;

- role modelling of required behaviours;

- rewarding wanted behaviours.

DEVELOPING GROUP LEARNING

Group learning may be developed by applying individual learning processes to groups and through team development activities. The development of group learning will enable the group to improve its performance. It involves activities such as:

- identifying learning styles;

- identifying group roles;

- developing communication skills;

- developing goal setting and action planning.

Identifying learning styles

The Honey and Mumford model of learning styles which was presented in Chapter 3 may be applied in a team situation. Each member of the team identifies their preferred learning style and an audit is carried out to identify the preferred learning styles of the team. This is simple to carry out and results in a chart such as the example given in Figure 5.2. This information may then be used by the group to explore and develop its working patterns.

Do this with managers

Figure 5.2.
TEAM LEARNING STYLES

	Theorist	Reflector	Activist	Pragmatist
Jane			1	2
Richard			2	1
John	1		2	
Bob	1	2		
Helen			1	2
Peter			1	2
Mike			2	1

1 refers to their preferred learning style. 2 is their secondary style.

In this team, the overall preferred learning style is activist followed by pragmatist.

A sales team working in a small company identified its preferred learning style as activist. As a team they were successful but frequently wasted a lot of time on projects which did not yield the expected results. The team reflected on this finding (this was facilitated by an outsider). They identified their tendency to rush into projects without much thought or research and they action-planned to build research and reflection time into their regular activities.

A systems development team based in a university identified their team learning styles as being predominantly reflector/theorist. After much reflection, they identified that as a team they needed to spend less time thinking and planning about the next project and actually do it. This matched with the feedback they got from their internal customers who continually complained that they spent too much time thinking about things and too little time delivering the goods.

Identifying group roles

Many group development activities involve identifying and understanding the roles that individuals adopt while working in a group. The group role is different from a functional role, e.g. someone's functional role may be as an accountant and their team role may be to co-ordinate and encourage different individuals' activities. There are a number of different approaches to exploring group or team roles.

One of the best known approaches is that developed by Meredith Belbin who developed his model by identifying the characteristics of successful teams. He identifies nine different roles in a group and these are outlined in Figure 5.3. If a team identifies its profile in terms of Belbin's model, then it enables staff to appreciate their strengths and also accept the weaknesses in each other. Gaps may be identified, which may then be addressed by the structuring of different activities or processes and the use of external support.

This approach may be used to help team members to identify their preferred roles and a standard inventory exists which may be completed by all group members. A computerised version is also available. Alternatively, observers may be asked to identify the preferred roles group members play during a particular activity or project.

This information may then be shared and a profile identified for the whole group. This is useful as a basis for discussing the team's current strengths and weaknesses and for identifying future actions.

> The Belbin inventory (Figure 5.3) was used with the senior management team of a voluntary organisation. They identified a lack of the following roles in their team: plant, shaper. They discussed this finding and noted that it related to a recent drop in income and the apparent drying up of ideas. They identified a range of strategies to make up these deficiencies.

appendix 3 .

Figure 5.3.
BELBIN TEAM ROLES

Role	Description	Allowable weaknesses
Plant	Creative, imaginative, unorthodox. Often able to solve difficult problems.	Weak in communicating ideas
Resource investigator	Extrovert, good communicator, enthusiastic, explores possibilities, enjoys networking	Easily gets bored
Co-ordinator	Co-ordinates group, enables different people to fully participate, clarifies goals, facilitates decision making, ensures activities progress	May not come up with the best ideas
Shaper	Dynamic, extrovert, wants to see results, finds ways around obstacles	Impatient, short-tempered
Monitor–evaluator	Carefully weighs up possibilities, makes sober judgements from evidence	Lacks enthusiasm
Teamworker	Sociable, builds relationships, reduces conflict, listens to colleagues' problems	Lacks clarity, may be indecisive
Implementer	Very disciplined, reliable, conservative, follows and develops new procedures	May be inflexible, sometimes slow to respond to new opportunities
Completer	Carries out all the correct procedures, checks for errors and omissions, ensures the task is completed on time	Anxious, finds it difficult to delegate
Specialist	Provides specialist knowledge or skills, dedicated and single minded.	Contributes on a very narrow front

Developing communication skills

Peter Senge has identified two key approaches to developing team communication and learning; these are the practices of dialogue and discussion.

- **Dialogue** involves 'deep listening' where the listener suspends their own ideas and judgements, and focuses on exploring and understanding the issue and its complexities.

- **Discussion** involves presenting and defending different views and searching for the 'best' idea which will then be used to move the matter forward.

Teams are frequently unaware of whether they are involved in dialogue or discussion, and which is most appropriate to a particular context. Traditionally, team activity is often focused on discussion and this is carried out in a competitive manner – 'the best man wins'. This does not necessarily lead to the most productive outcome.

Dialogue and discussion are complementary activities which require the skills of reflection, surfacing and public examination of mental models. Mental models or maps are the internal maps everyone has of their world and these have been created by generalising, deleting and distorting information. Mental models are personally tailored maps of the world and include values and beliefs. They are very important as they enable a person to be able to behave without making a decision about every little detail.

For example, this approach was used by two managers who were in conflict about 'the proper way' to organise team meetings. One manager's mental model of the world included the belief that 'everyone should speak at meetings' and this resulted in the behaviour that she opened up opportunities for team members to speak during meetings. She didn't make a conscious decision to invite different people to speak as it has become a habitual behaviour. Her colleague had the belief that 'we are all adults and can look after ourselves' and so didn't facilitate

> space for quiet colleagues to speak up during meetings. A *dialogue* between these two managers and their teams enabled them to understand and accommodate each other's style and reduced the friction between them.

However, some habitual behaviours may be unhelpful or inappropriate to a particular situation. The ability to explore and perhaps update mental models is likely to increase the capability of an individual to act in a flexible manner. Attempts to surface and explore these maps frequently leads to defensive behaviours. Unless the people concerned are skilled in reflecting, asking questions and gently surfacing mental models, they are unlikely to facilitate change.

It is very difficult for someone to develop their mental models without the help of their colleagues, as this activity involves surfacing unconscious or deeply held ideas of which their owner may be unaware.

Developing goal setting and action planning

The skills of goal setting and action planning are best developed through practice. Goals are achievable outcomes and a common method of developing group goal setting is to use the SMART approach. SMART goals are those which are:

• Specific;

• Measurable;

• Achievable;

• Realistic;

• Time-bound.

The development of group goals can be facilitated in group training or work-based sessions, where a team is asked to identify their goals for a particular time period. They may generate a list of 10–20 possible goals. From this list, 5 goals are identified as being priorities.

These goals may then be translated into individual, small group or whole team action plans which cover the following issues:

• What will you do? Be SMART.

• What resources will you need to do it?

• What support will you need to do it?

• When will you have completed your activity?

• How will you obtain feedback from your activity?

• Who will check progress and review activity with you?

One of the key factors when developing goal setting and action planning is to enable the staff to develop their own goals and 'own' their action plans. In some situations, action plans which relate to learning activities are called learning contracts. Both action plans and learning contracts may be signed by the interested parties. An example action plan is presented in Figure 4.2.

A small food company wanted to increase the amount of incidental learning from everyday workplace events. The training officer organised a half day training programme which focused on learning from experience and using action plans. At the end of the workshop, individual staff completed action plans and these covered the following activities:

• obtain feedback from production engineer on her view of weekly cleansing operation;
• spend 15 minutes every day reviewing meetings with disgruntled staff, identify and act on common themes;
• ask colleague for feedback every day;
• arrange for a student from the local university to work in the company for work placement for 4 weeks;
• come in during night shift and obtain feedback from night time operatives.

6

Developing organisational learning

INTRODUCTION

chapter 2.

In this chapter the focus is on developing learning at an organisational level. While individual and team learning will help to improve the quality of learning, activities also need to take place at the organisational level if there is to be significant development of whole organisation learning.

The use of goal setting and action planning to facilitate the alignment of individual and organisational goals is described in the next section. This is followed by an exploration of ways in which managers may develop a learning environment in their organisation. Research work by Peter Honey has identified four types of activities – role model, provider, system builder and champion – which all managers need to carry out to develop a learning environment.

The next section explores two approaches to developing learning organisations: continuous and discontinuous activities. Continuous activities are those which are part of a long-term process such as working towards Investors in People, while discontinuous activities are one-off events which serve to maintain momentum and introduce new or different ideas into the long term development activities. Both types of activity are required in the development of a learning organisation.

The next section explores a range of ideas which Pearn and his co-workers have learnt from their extensive experience of helping organisations develop into becoming learning ones. These ideas are included as they present a useful checklist which managers and change agents may want to use to learn from the experiences of others.

This section is followed by a self-assessment questionnaire, which readers may like to complete to identify the factors in their organisation which facilitate learning.

INDIVIDUAL, TEAM AND ORGANISATIONAL GOAL SETTING

In a learning organisation, the organisation leaders are likely to facilitate a process which results in:

• an organisational vision;

• organisational goals;

• departmental/team goals;

• individual goals.

The organisational vision may be developed, in the first instance, by the leaders and then developed over time by input from staff at all levels. Organisational goals are frequently developed by groups of senior managers and then translated into departmental or team goals through discussion and negotiation with groups of staff. Individual goals may then be negotiated during one-to-one meetings with staff and their managers.

The goals are then translated into a series of objectives which may be achieved by successfully completing one or more actions. These are planned through the action planning process described at the end of Chapter 4. A sample action plan form is presented in Figure 4.2.

Example of organisational goal setting and action planning activity

A housing association expanded rapidly over a two-year period and developed from a staffing base of 50 to 110 staff. The senior management team led by the Chief Executive wanted to:

• encourage team working;
• re-motivate staff;
• re-focus organisational development activities;
• re-focus individual development activities.

They decided to achieve this through a series of team training events which would be attended by all staff within the organisation. They

---

decided to integrate team building and goal setting/action planning processes through a series of 2-day events. These were facilitated by two consultants and each event included the following activities:

- identifying the strengths and weaknesses of team working;

- analysis and discussion of team roles using the Belbin inventory;

- brainstorming team goals for the next 12 months;

- listing the team goals in the order of priority and identifying the top 5 goals;

- the top 5 goals were then analysed and, where appropriate, listed as a set of even more specific tasks;

- each individual then selected, identified and action planned one or more goals or tasks;

- pairs of staff then selected, identified and action planned one or more goals or tasks;

- whole teams then selected, identified and action planned one or more goals or tasks;

- at each stage, staff shared their work and intentions with their colleagues.

This process resulted in individuals and teams developing action plans in a supportive environment. Actions planned included:

- explore and, if appropriate, obtain mobile telephones for maintenance staff;

- set up a new working party to evaluate the current IT systems;

- register for a part time MBA;

- arrange a social event each month.

A follow-up event was held three months later and staff shared their achievements and amended their action plans in response to new developments. The whole process resulted in a highly motivated workforce and a great deal of enthusiasm for moving forward in a planned manner.

DEVELOPING A LEARNING ENVIRONMENT

Peter Honey (Honey and Mumford, 1996) describes a learning environment as one in which:

the behaviours and practices involved in continuous development are actively encouraged.

A learning environment is achieved through shared action by individuals and groups at every level:

- **individual staff** – take responsibility for their own learning and development;

- **one-to-one relationships** with other people – provide the opportunity for validating and extending individual learning;

- **teams** – encourage group learning and share and develop individual learning;

- **whole organisation** – encourages and integrates learning from all staff (individually, in one-to-one relationships, and in teams) for the benefit of all the staff and the organisation.

Peter Honey describes four key sets of activities which managers need to carry out in order to develop a learning environment:

- **role model** – managers need to role model in their behaviour and actions that they are learners;

- **provider** – managers need to consciously plan and provide learning opportunities for other people and actively encourage and support them while they are learning;

- **system builder** – learning needs to be built into the organisation's processes and be explicitly on the agenda;

- **champion** – managers needs to champion the importance of learning for their team, other parts of the organisation and the organisation as a whole.

Role model

In a survey of 250 managers, Peter Honey discovered that the most frequent role model behaviours are:

- identifying and seizing learning opportunities as they arise;

- communicating what they have learnt;

- asking questions, challenging currently accepted beliefs or methods, suggesting ideas for improvement;

- using an ongoing personal development plan;

- review/learn from their mistakes.

Provider

The most common provider behaviours are:

- coaching staff to maintain and improve their performance;

- encouraging staff to adopt 'learning' behaviours such as asking questions, experimenting, reviewing successes and mistakes;

- briefing/de-briefing staff before/after a learning activity to help them learn more;

- giving help and encouragement to learn when things go wrong.

System builder

In Peter Honey's survey of 250 managers, he discovered that the most frequent system builder activity was:

- using a process for agreeing and reviewing learning contracts/personal development plans with my people.

This was followed by the next most frequent items of:

- using formal processes for generating feedback on performance (upwards, downwards, sideways);

- safeguarding the learning and development budget.

Champion

Champions of learning tend to:

- point out the penalties the organisation incurs through a lack of learning, e.g. same mistakes, wheels reinvented, best people leave due to a lack of developmental opportunities;

- encourage people from different groups/functions/parts of the organisation to meet to exchange ideas/experiences/lessons learned;

- use a variety of communication channels to disseminate the learning message.

The development of a learning organisation is an ongoing process which is never completed. Managers need to constantly create and re-create learning environments for their staff. One of the most challenging tasks managers are likely to face is maintaining their commitment to becoming a learning organisation when they face particularly difficult challenges. In these difficult situations, people tend to respond by attempting to take control and dictate outcomes rather than facilitating activities in a manner which empowers their workers and enables them to be innovative and creative.

CONTINUOUS AND DISCONTINUOUS DEVELOPMENT ACTIVITIES

Learning organisations are likely to be involved in a range of long-term continuous processes as well as short-term discontinuous or 'one-off' activities which are all focused on helping to improve the quality of learning by individuals and teams within the organisation. Examples of continuous developments include:

- working towards Investors in People;

- working towards ISO 9000;

- planned skills training on topics such as: assertiveness techniques; goal setting; learning strategies; time management; stress management; multisensory learning strategies;

- human resource management tools such as: employees' development processes; progress/performance review; appraisal, individual development plans;

- action learning sets and quality circles;

- benchmarking best practice.

These activities help to build the underlying systems, processes and skills in the organisation and provide valuable information which help the organisation to grow and develop. They also help to develop and nurture an environment in which planned growth and development is seen as positive.

Discontinuous approaches to development are a means by which unusual or different activities may be introduced, perhaps as a one-off event, for the purposes of:

- maintaining and raising staff enthusiasm and motivation;

- helping staff to develop their creativity;

- developing new and innovative approaches to solving problems.

Examples of discontinuous activities include:

- one-off events such as: inspirational talk by world leader in a relevant field; an away day in a unique setting; a weekend trip which involves the outdoors;

- inviting children or young people to visit or work in the organisation and report their findings;

- use of accelerated learning techniques as a part of organisational activities such as: aromatherapy during meetings; group mind mapping for problem solving; introduction of appropriate physical exercise during staff development sessions or meetings.

Examples of the use of unusual activities to support the development of a learning organisation include:

- *Culture Club*

  In a university learning services department (made up of library, IT and media staff), a lunchtime Culture Club was established as an informal means of empowering staff to improve their working environment. These lunchtime sessions involve skills training on topics such as: giving positive feedback, making changes within my circle of influence, managing negativity positively and they also provide a forum for developing new ideas and initiatives. They enabled managers and staff from the five different university sites to meet and work together outside the normal 'line management' system.

- *Parenting workshops*

  A number of schools have established workshops which support parents and guardians who want to help their children learn. These workshops may cover subjects such as: individual learning styles; revision techniques; improving memory; helping with projects; mind mapping and others. Some organisations have started to develop parenting workshops as a means of supporting their employees who are involved with young people and also as a means of enhancing the employers' own ability to learn.

- *Unusual diagnostic tools*

  A marketing company decided to analyse their internal processes and activities using a new diagnostic technique, which was based on the ideas expounded in the field of neurolinguistic programming. They analysed their processes and activities from the perspectives of vision, sound and feeling and linking these with individual learning styles (see

Chapter 3). They discovered that all their internal processes were biased towards auditory processes and they decided to build in more visual stimuli through the use of diagrams, charts and visual displays in their offices. They found these results surprising as in their field they were well known for their imaginative multisensory products and, on reflection, they realised that their everyday internal activities were extremely one dimensional and uninspiring. As a result of adding these dimensions to their internal processes, e.g. project management processes, they discovered that their output increased and that the amount of discord between staff decreased.

LEARNING FROM EXPERIENCE

Pearn and his co-workers, writing in 1995, have identified a range of lessons which they have learnt from their experiences of helping to develop learning organisations. These are:

Involve the people most affected at the earliest possible stage

In a large organisation this may mean involving representatives from different groups of people rather than all the affected people. In a small or medium-sized organisation it may be possible to involve everyone. Sometimes people are not involved because 'they don't have the appropriate skills' or 'the situation is too complex' or 'they don't understand the big picture'. In these cases, it may be necessary to install a learning process so that everyone can be involved in the development processes.

Champions for a learning organisation need to understand how they and other people learn

In order to influence others and develop a 'learning for all' ethos, champions and change-makers need to have a good understanding of how they learn (and their learning weaknesses or blindspots) and also how others learn. The ideas of people such as Peter Honey and Alan Mumford (described in Chapter 3) are useful in helping to understand some of the complexities of learning. Champions and change-makers need to be congruent in what they say and do with regard to implementing learning in their organisation. They also need to recognise themselves as learners, i.e. they are not 'special'.

Diagnostic and analytical processes are crucial

Diagnostic tools and analytical processes are an essential part of organisational development processes as they enable objective information to be collected on different activities, processes and people. If these are repeated over time, then they enable a time series to be built up.

> For example, a Training and Enterprise Council used an organisational culture diagnostic tool every two years. The results from these diagnoses were presented on a large wall chart which was displayed in the human resources department. These clearly demonstrated a change from a bureaucratic culture to a task-orientated and people-centred culture. Staff found the diagnostic tool products useful as they offered an external perspective on their organisation which validated the change processes which had been put in place.

Managers must see facilitating learning as a prime activity

Facilitating learning is a prime activity for managers and is an essential pre-requisite for the development of a learning organisation. Managers must not only facilitate their own learning but also facilitate that of their staff.

Evolution is better than prescription

Every organisation is unique and is more likely to be successful if it learns for itself and grows in its own way. Guides such as this report offer an overview of the territory rather than a detailed set of prescriptions which must be followed precisely.

Break down the barriers between the managers and the 'managed'

The barriers between the managers and the 'managed' mean that there is an artificial barrier to problem-solving, decision-making and creativity. Frequently, managers or their staff keep information or ideas secret because they feel they are unacceptable or may 'rock the boat'. Analysis of serious mistakes in organisations often show that different people within the organisation were aware of the problem but did not speak up for a variety of reasons. Breaking down this barrier helps to develop learning activities and improves the quality of information, ideas and creativity in the whole organisation.

The learning organisation is a quest not an end state

While there are many examples of organisations which strive to become learning ones, it is a state to which they aspire and will never reach. Moving along this route offers the opportunity to develop the learning of individuals and teams, and as a result, work towards achieving the goals of the organisation. Continuous changes both in the external environment and also within the organisation (e.g. the departure of staff and new recruits) means that there are always new challenges and new approaches to learning for everyone.

The business case for becoming a learning organisation should be supported by a vision and values that inspire

Sometimes champions of learning organisations forget the reasons for this form of development, i.e. it is to help the business achieve its goals in both the short and the long term. The reasons and benefits for the development of a learning organisation need to be accepted and internalised by everyone if it is not to be ignored or seen as the current management flavour of the month.

The development processes toward becoming a learning organisation enable individual, team and organisational goals, values and beliefs to become aligned so that there is a coherence and integrity in all the organisational activities. This synergy enables individuals and the business to achieve their goals.

Mystique busting is essential

The idea of the learning organisation is growing constantly and associated with it is a set of jargon. An increasing number of consultants and management development agencies are offering sometimes complicated processes and activities to help an organisation improve their learning capacity. This mystique is unhelpful as it disempowers individuals from developing their own ability to learn and to share that within their teams and organisations. Where individuals set themselves up as experts on learning organisations, then they are immediately setting up divisions and are disempowering their colleagues within their organisation. The basic ideas behind a learning organisation are simple and can be internalised by everyone.

Empowerment

The empowerment of everyone within the organisation is a crucial factor in the development of a learning organisation. Individuals need to be equipped with a range of skills, e.g. learning skills, decision making and assertiveness skills, if they are to become empowered.

Review and reflection

Many organisations have a culture which is based on reaction and quick action. This does not help the development of learning processes, where review and reflection are necessary steps if individuals, teams and the organisation are to learn from their successes and mistakes.

Fitting interventions to the organisation

Some organisations obtain 'off-the shelf' intervention processes to help them develop as a learning organisation. The application of these processes in this way may be of limited value as they do not encourage individuals and teams to tailor-make the learning activities to suit themselves and their own stage in development. These management tools often assume that there is a 'right way' to develop a learning organisation, while the reality is that each organisation must develop its own way and learn from their successes and mistakes.

CONCLUDING THOUGHTS

This report has drawn together a range of theoretical and practical ideas, which focus on helping an organisation to move towards becoming a learning organisation. The crucial factor in developing a learning organisation is to develop individuals' learning skills and to see learning as a key organisational activity. As an organisation develops, the responsibility for learning shifts from individual managers and the human resources department to become everyone's responsibility. Once this starts to happen, then a learning organisation is developing.

CHECKLIST OF FACTORS WHICH FACILITATE LEARNING

Please place a tick in the box which most matches the situation in your unit, department or organisation. You may wish to photocopy this questionnaire and ask your colleagues to complete it too.

	Not true	True to some extent	Generally true
In my unit, department or organisation: individuals			
Are encouraged to learn new skills	❏	❏	❏
Are encouraged to ask questions	❏	❏	❏
Are encouraged to share their learning	❏	❏	❏
Take charge of their own learning	❏	❏	❏
Have an individual learning contract/ development plan	❏	❏	❏
Support their colleagues in their learning activities	❏	❏	❏
In my unit, department or organisation: teams			
Are motivated to learn	❏	❏	❏
Are encouraged to make time to reflect on and learn from their actions	❏	❏	❏
Spend time on reviewing their team working and learning processes	❏	❏	❏
Invite others, e.g. consultants, trainers to observe them in action and feedback their findings	❏	❏	❏
Are open about their mistakes and share learning about them	❏	❏	❏
Celebrate their successes as a team	❏	❏	❏
In my unit, department or organisation: managers			
Are motivated to learn new skills	❏	❏	❏
Are encouraged to share their learning	❏	❏	❏
Are receptive to new ideas	❏	❏	❏
Take charge of their own learning	❏	❏	❏
Have an individual learning contract/ development plan	❏	❏	❏
Support their colleagues in their learning activities	❏	❏	❏
Arrange learning activities such as training events, coaching, mentoring	❏	❏	❏
View mistakes as learning opportunities	❏	❏	❏

The more ticks are in the right-hand column, the more learning is facilitated in your organisation.

7

Resources

SPECIFIC TOOLS

Allan, B., Cook, M. and Lewis, R. (1996) *The Independent Learner: Developing Independence in Learning*, University of Lincolnshire and Humberside.

This booklet contains an inventory for developing independent learners.

Honey, P. and Mumford, A. (1996) *How to Manage your Learning Environment*, Peter Honey, Maidenhead.

This is a down-to-earth manual which provides managers with a range of practical activities which help them to develop and sustain a learning environment at work.

Honey, P. and Mumford, A. (1995) *101 Ways to Develop Your People, Without Really Trying*, Peter Honey, Maidenhead.

This book is packed with ideas which may be used by any manager in any organisation to help people learn and develop.

Honey, P. (1995) *Manual of Self-Assessment Questionnaires*, Peter Honey, Maidenhead.

This binder contains 21 questionnaires to improve personal effectiveness. The questionnaires are grouped into the following sections: assertiveness; attitudes and emotions; behaviour styles; creative thinking; learning and self-development; solving people-problems; teamwork; trainer competence.

Honey, P. and Mumford, A. (1992) *The Manual of Learning Styles*, Peter Honey, Maidenhead.

This manual contains: descriptions of the learning cycle and the four learning styles – activist, reflector, theorist and pragmatist; the Learning Styles Questionnaire; a variety of norms against which results can be compared; suggestions for trainers.

Mayo, A. and Lank, E. (1994) *The Power of Learning: a Guide to Gaining a Competitive Advantage*, Institute of Personnel and Development, London.

This book provides a practical overview of learning organisations and their development. It includes a practical self-assessment tool which will help any kind of organisation to benchmark itself against a learning organisation.

Pearn, M. and Mulrooney, C. (1995) *Tools for a Learning Organisation*, Institute of Personnel and Development, London.

This set of four workbooks provides a useful set of resources (checklists, inventories and exercises) which may be used in organisational development activities.

REFERENCES

Allan, B., Cook, M. and Lewis, R. (1996) *The Independent Learner: Developing Independence in Learning*, University of Lincolnshire and Humberside.

Argyris, C. (1978) *Organisational Learning*, Addison-Wesley, Harlow.

Argyris, C. (1990) *Overcoming Organisational Defences: Facilitating Organisational Learning*, Allyn and Bacon, Boston.

Ball, C. (1991) *Learning Pays: The Role of Post-Compulsory Education and Training*, Royal Society of Arts, London.

Ball, C. (1992) *Profitable Learning*, Royal Society of Arts, London.

Beckhard, R. and Pritchard, W. (1992) *Changing the Essence: The Art of Creating and Leading Fundamental Change in Organisations*, Jossey-Bass, London.

Belbin, M. (1981) *Management Teams: Why They Succeed or Fail*, Butterworth, London.

Casey, D. (1993) *Managing Learning in Organisations*, Open Unviersity, Milton Keynes.

Cunningham, I. (1994) *The Wisdom of Strategic Learning*, McGraw-Hill, London.

Garratt, B. (1994) *The Learning Organisation*, Harper Collins, London.

Hayes, R. H., Wheelwright, S. C. and Clark, K. B. (1988) *Dynamic Manufacturing: Creating the Learning Organisation*, The Free Press, New York.

Honey, P. (1982) *The Manual of Learning Styles*, Peter Honey, Maidenhead.

Honey, P. (1991) *The Learning Organisation Simplified*. Training and development, pp. 30–33, Peter Honey, Maidenhead.

Honey, P. (1994) *101 Ways to Develop Your People, Without Really Trying*, Peter Honey, Maidenhead.

Honey, P. (1994) *Learning Log: A Way of Enhancing Learning From Experience*, Peter Honey, Maidenhead.

Jones, A. M. and Hendry, C. (1992) *The Learning Organisation: A Review of Literature and Practice*, HRD Partnership, London.

Kincheloe, J. L. (1991) *Teachers as Researchers: Qualitative Enquiry as a Path to Empowerment*, Falmer, London.

Kolb, D. A. (1984) *Experiential Learning: Experience as the Source of Learning and Development*. Prentice-Hall, Englewood Cliffs, N. J.

Lewis, R. (1996) *The Learning Organisation*, Brainwaves, Spring. Centre for Learning, Hull.

Lewis, R. and Allan, B. (1996) *The Independent Learner: An Overview*, University of Lincolnshire and Humberside.

Mabey, C. and Iles, P. (1994) *Managing Learning*, Routledge, London.

Mayo, A. and Lank, E. (1994) *The Power of Learning*, IPD, London.

O'Connor, J. and McDermott, I. (1996) *Principles of NLP*, Thorsons, London.

O'Connor, J. and Seymour, J. (1993) *Introducing Neuro-Linguistic Programming*, Aquarian, London.

Ostrander, S. and Schroeder, L. (1994) *Superlearning 2000*, Souvenir, London.

Pearn, M., Roderick, C. and Mulrooney, C. (1995) *Learning Organisations in Practice*, McGraw-Hill, London.

Pedler, M., Burgoyne, J. and Boydell, T. (1992) *The Learning Organisation*, McGraw-Hill, London.

Pedler, M., Burgoyne, J., Boydell, T. and Welshman, G. (1990) *Self-Development in Organisations*, McGraw-Hill, London.

Senge, P. (1990) *The Fifth Discipline*, Century, London.

Senge, P. (1994) *The Fifth Discipline Fieldbook*, Century, London.